Jobs People Do

Christopher Maynard

DK

DORLING KINDERSLEY
LONDON • NEW YORK • STUTTGART • MOSCOW

DK

A DORLING KINDERSLEY BOOK

Text Christopher Maynard
Project Editor Penny Smith
Art Editor Claire Penny
Deputy Managing Art Editor Jane Horne
Deputy Managing Editor Mary Ling
DTP Designer Nicola Studdart
Production Kate Oliver
Picture Researcher James Clarke
Photography Steve Gorton, Dave King,
Ray Moller

Additional photography by Paul Bricknell,
Geoff Brighling, Andy Crawford, Michael
Crockett, Philip Dowell, Mike Dunning, Lynton
Gardiner, John Garrett, Philip Gatward, Frank
Greenaway, Kit Houghton, Dave Icing, Colin
Keates, Bob Lang Rish, Richard Leeney, Tim
Ridley, Jules Selmes, Steve Shott, Chris Stevens,
Clive Streeter, Colin Walton, Alex Wilson,
Peter Wilson

First published in Great Britain in 1997
by Dorling Kindersley Limited,
9 Henrietta Street, London WC2E 8PS
Visit us on the World Wide Web at http://www.dk.com

A CIP catalogue record for this book is available
from the British Library.

ISBN: 0-7513-5518-6

Colour reproduction by Colourscan
Printed and bound in Italy by Mondadori

The publisher would like to thank the following for their
kind permission to reproduce their photographs:

t=top, b=bottom, l=left, r=right, c=centre,
BC=back cover, FC=front cover
John Birdsall: 28tl; **Britstock-IFA**: 5c; E. Bach 31cb;
Exeter Maritime Museum 10cl; **Robert Harding Picture
Library**: 8bc, 9tl, 9c, 12tl, 25bl; **David Hoffman**: 13tr;
The Image Bank: Barros & Barros 6tl; Jeff Cadge 20cb;
G. Colliva 16tl; Ocean Images Inc 11bl; Terje Rakke 11tl,
31ca; Michael Salas 24tl; Alvis Upitus 18cl; Weinberg
Clark 18bl; **Images**: 7tl **L.A.T. Photographic**: 29bl, 29tl;
Magnum Photos: B. Barbey 19cb; **Pictor**: 7c, 9bl, 10bc,
11cl, 14tl, 17bl, 22c; ©**Renault**: 29c; **Rex**: 8c, 23bl; Sipa
Press 5tr; **Tony Stone Images**: 22tl, 30tl; Bruce Ayres 6bl,
7bl, 26bc; Brian Blauser 4c; Paul Chesley 17tl; Robert E.
Daemrich 13cl; Charles Gupton 8tl; Frank Herholdt 21cb;
Bruno de Hogues 16cb; Kevin Horan 28tr; Arnulf Husmo
10c, 27c; Patrick Ingrand 16bl; Fernand Ivaldi 15tr; Chris
Kaporka 16cl; Richard Kaylin 4tl; Alan Klehr 27bl;
Jonathan Nourok 25cl; Steve Outram 10clb; Tony Page
28cl; Jon Riley 26tr; Michael Rosenfeld 15cla, 21tl, 28bl;
Andy Sacks 23ca; Michael Thersiquel 10tl; Bob Thomas
12tr; Richard Todd 22bl; Tom & Pat Valenti 14bl; Terry
Vine 14cb; Mark Wagner 17c; **Telegraph Colour Library**:
7bc, 13cb, 18tl, 20tl, 21cl, 25tr, 26c; L. Lefkowitz 6tc; Tony
Ward 15c; Neal Wilson 6cl; ©**Wake-Upp Productions**:
Gérard Planchenault 29cl; **Zefa**: 20cla, 24cl, 24c

In addition, Dorling Kindersley would like to thank the
following people and organisations for their assistance in
the production of this book:
Barbara Owen (for making outfits); Bonpoint, Moss Bros
(for clothes); Ocean Leisure (for diving equipment); Hollie
Almeida, Cameron Blundell, Holly Franklin, Cameron
Nisbett, Alexander Peter, Siána Scott, Rachelle See, Lauren
Shons, Matthew Stahl, Shana Swash, Natasha Tuke, Sahil
Udhian, John Vella, Peter Vella (for modelling)

Contents

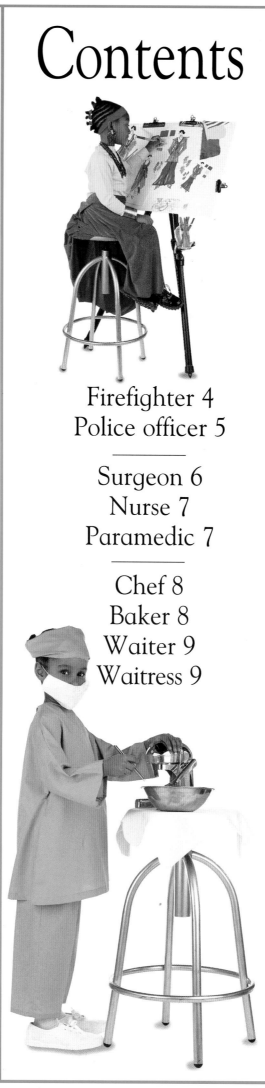

Firefighter

Airport emergency
Airport fires are fought with foam. It quickly smothers flames so fuel tanks aren't set alight.

I am a firefighter and my job is to put out fires and to save people from burning buildings. When there is an emergency, I quickly put on my fireproof clothes, jump in the fire truck, and race to the scene. Then I soak the blaze with water or foam.

Helmet to protect head and neck.

Fire axe to break open doors.

Safety clothing
Firefighters are protected from sparks by their wide-brimmed helmets and long coats.

Putting out a fire
Powerful jets of water are pumped from hoses. Fires can then be fought from a safe distance.

Clothing made of material that won't burn or melt.

Fireproof boots tipped with steel.

Ladder truck
The ladder is used to fight fire in tall buildings, and it pulls out up to three times the length shown above. Switches and handles on the side of the truck control the ladder, water gun, and hoses.

Police officer

I am a police officer so I protect people from robbers and burglars. When a crime is committed, I interview witnesses and try to find out who to arrest. When there is a road accident I get the traffic flowing again. Every day as I patrol my beat, I talk to local people so that I can find out what is going on.

Walkie-talkie radio to stay in touch with headquarters.

Handling crowds
The police control crowds so members of the public don't block traffic, or get trampled and hurt.

Patrol bike
Highway patrol police have fast motorcycles to get through traffic blocking busy roads.

Patrol car
The lights on this car flash and sirens scream to keep people out of its way as it races to a crime.

Road safety
All children must learn how to cross the road safely. A local police officer may take them out and show them how to use a pedestrian crossing properly.

Mounted patrol
Police sometimes patrol on big, well-trained horses. When they are near crowds they can see over all the heads, and if any trouble starts they can signal to each other.

Surgeon

Bare bones
X-ray pictures let doctors see inside the body.

I am a doctor and I work in a hospital as a surgeon. I use tools, such as scalpels, to operate on patients and cure diseased or injured organs. Patients are given drugs called anaesthetics, so they sleep comfortably while I am at work.

Germ barrier
Surgeons wear face masks so they don't spread germs.

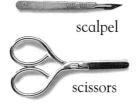

scalpel

scissors

mask

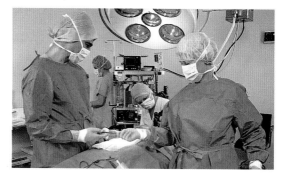

In the theatre
Teams of surgeons work in very clean rooms called operating theatres. Here they fix broken legs, take out tonsils, and repair bodies damaged in traffic accidents.

stethoscope

Being examined
Family doctors may examine you in their surgery, or come to your home if you are particularly ill. A stethoscope helps them to hear if anything is wrong with your heart.

Nurse

In hospital
Nurses check patients in turn. Parents can stay with their sick children in hospital.

antiseptic cream

thermometer

medicine

bandages

I am a nurse in a hospital. When people are ill, they rest and get better on the ward where I work. I care for them by making them comfortable in bed. I also give them pills and injections that the doctor has prescribed.

air ambulance

Paramedic

I am a paramedic and I treat people at the scene of an accident. Then I put them on a stretcher and take them to hospital in an ambulance.

Passing on information
Nurses keep notes on their patients. Then other nurses can check that the patients have had their medicine.

First aid
In an emergency, paramedics check to see if the person is breathing. Sometimes they give oxygen through a mask.

Say ahh
If a pupil doesn't feel well, the school nurse may check for a high or low temperature using a thermometer.

vegetables

Chef

In the kitchen
All the ingredients are prepared early in the day. This way chefs can cook quickly, so customers don't have to wait long for their meal to arrive.

I am a chef and I run my own restaurant. Every morning, bright and early, I go to the market to buy fresh food. Back in my kitchen, I chop and slice ingredients, put casseroles in the oven to cook, and desserts in the fridge to set. I often work until late at night, cooking and serving up food.

Baker

I am a baker and I work in a busy bakery. I make white and brown loaves and rolls, and dozens of delicious tarts and cakes. I start very early in the morning, so people can come and buy hot, fresh bread from me when they get up.

Looking good
Restaurant food must taste good, but it is just as important that it looks good too. Chefs learn at college how to decorate and present their food.

Hot from the oven
Bakers cook hundreds of loaves each week. The bread turns golden brown when it is cooked.

basket of bread

Waiter

I am a waiter and I serve food in a luxurious restaurant. I set the tables with cutlery, plates, and glasses. Then, when customers arrive, I show them to their tables. I give them the menu and write down their orders on my pad. When their food is ready, I serve it to them. Later I clear away the dirty plates and present the bill.

corkscrew

Eating out
Some restaurants have terraces and customers can eat outside. Waiters are busy all day, pouring drinks and serving meals to guests.

Waitress

I am a waitress and I work in a smart hotel. During the afternoons I serve coffee and tea, and lots of beautifully decorated little cakes. I am always polite to my customers.

Wine and dine
Tables at grand restaurants have to be booked in advance. The food and wine is very expensive.

What can I get you?
Waiters often speak several languages so they can talk to customers from different countries. They discuss the menu and suggest dishes the chef does well.

Set the table
Waiters know how to set tables with the right knives, forks, and spoons for each course.

Landing fish
When the boat docks, the fish are unloaded and packed in ice to keep them fresh.

Pot once used for catching lobsters.

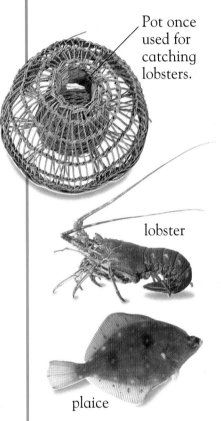

lobster

plaice

The fish market
Fish are sorted into boxes, then they are sold to shops and restaurants.

fisherman's boots

Fisherwoman

I am a fisherwoman and I catch fish for people to eat. I drop nets over the sides of my boat, pull in hundreds of fish, and store them until I reach land. It can be cold and rough at sea, but I love being on the water.

At sea
Fishing boats are small, and packed with nets and tackle. They can withstand gentle waves, but return to land if a bad storm approaches.

Mending nets
Fishing nets get torn at sea, so there are always plenty of repairs for the crew to do when they are not fishing.

Hat keeps off the wind and spray.

Rubber boots keep feet dry.

Diver

I am a deep-sea diver.
I wear a wet suit every time
I dive. This is because deep
down under the water it
is very cold. I carry oxygen
tanks so that I can breathe.
Sometimes I take tools
with me so I can do repairs.

Rig workers
Some divers are
based on oil rigs.
They work on
pipes and valves
under the sea.

Hidden treasure
Divers may look for treasure
in an ancient wreck or city
lost under the waves.

Undersea explorer
Submersibles are designed to dive
much deeper than humans. They
are used to explore the seabed.

Steel helmets
Divers wear helmets deep under the
ocean. These stop their heads getting
squashed by the pressure of the water.

goggles

oxygen
tank

flippers

Diving tools
A diver needs a
lot of equipment.
It includes:

watches

knife

gloves

torch

belt

diving boots

11

Photographer

I am a photographer and I take the pictures that you see in magazines and newspapers. Sometimes I photograph big parties and weddings, or I work in a studio with lights and a model. When I've got time, I like to develop my own film.

Moving pictures
Photographers take moving pictures for television or the cinema. They often film all over the world.

Working in a studio
Photographs are often taken in a studio. This is so the photographer can get exactly the right lighting effects.

flash

camera

film

lenses

Tools of the trade
Cameras can be fitted with a flash and lenses. They take bright or dark pictures, colour or black-and-white shots.

Sports photography
Newspaper photographers go to all the big sports events. They try to capture action shots, and use long lenses so they can get close-up pictures from far away.

A tripod keeps the camera steady.

Reporter

I work for a newspaper as a sports reporter. Every day I watch teams play and talk to the players. I ask them about the sport, about why they moved to a new team, or if they have been hurt. Then I type up the story on my computer. I have to work quickly – if I don't get my story in on time it won't be printed.

News of the day
Reporters cover all types of news, from celebrity weddings to political rallies.

TV news programmes
Reporters also work for TV news. Their stories are read to the camera by a news reader.

Getting quotes
Reporters try to talk directly to the people who make the news. The best reporters are the ones who tell both sides of a story.

Interviews
Whether working for radio or for a newspaper, reporters like to record their interviews. In this way they can be sure of what people say to them.

Teacher

I am a teacher and I teach a class of young children. They are lively but they work hard, and I like helping them to learn new things. I teach six different subjects. I like science best because I can show my class experiments to make them understand how the world works.

pencil

pen

compass

calculator

ruler

Parents' evening
Teachers discuss with parents how children are doing at school. They show examples of their class work.

Helping hand
Teachers explain things to the whole class, or they help just one child at a time. Learning to read and write are two of the most useful things children do.

Training
Children learn to play sports at school. They learn the rules of a game, and how to work together as a team. Running around also keeps their bodies fit and strong.

Story time
This is when the teacher reads the class a story and shows them the pictures. Children are encouraged to put up their hands if they want to ask a question.

Scientist

I am a scientist and I work in a laboratory. I test different chemicals, looking for ways to cure illness. If a chemical works, I make new drugs and test them carefully. I study how the drugs affect the human body. Once I am sure a drug is safe, it can be used by doctors to treat illness.

Close up
Microscopes are used to look at cells that are too small to be seen by the human eye.

Studying life
Some scientists study how plants grow. They search for ways to make better food, and crops that pests won't eat.

microscope

Palaeontologist

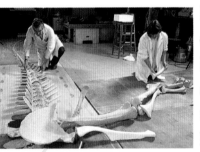

I am a rock scientist, or palaeontologist. I study rocks to find dinosaur fossils. I fit them together to see how dinosaurs looked.

trowels   hammers   sieve

Keeping track
Palaeontologists keep records of the fossils they discover to help work out their age. The oldest dinosaur fossils ever found are over 200 million years old.

Train driver

I am a train driver. Every day I take my train up and down the country, stopping at stations to pick up passengers. Sometimes I carry letters on my train too. As I drive along, I have to watch out for signals that tell me when it is safe to go and when I must stop. I always try to keep my train running on time.

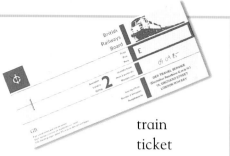

train ticket

Bullet trains
In Japan, super-trains are called bullet trains. This is because they have rounded fronts, just like bullets. They travel so fast that all the windows are sealed shut. If you could open them, the air would blast in like a hurricane.

Leaving Paris
French super-trains are called TGVs. Once they leave their station in Paris, they pick up speed until they are racing through the countryside at 300km/h. Drivers can make them go, stop, and reverse. The trains steer themselves along the railway tracks.

Fast driver
The controls of a TGV train look a lot like those on a passenger jet. The switches and dials tell the driver that the train is running safely, and that the line is clear.

Sitting comfortably
Passengers board their train from the station platform. Inside they are often served drinks and snacks at their seats, just like in a plane. On some trains there is a restaurant where people can eat dinner.

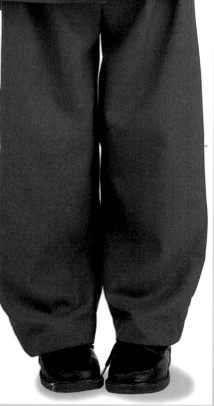

Pilot

I am a pilot and I fly planes from country to country. Sometimes I carry passengers and sometimes cargo. I know what all the dials in the cockpit mean, how to alter course, and how to put down the wheels for landing. I travel all over the world and often don't go home for weeks.

aeroplane

Directing traffic
Air traffic controllers make sure aeroplanes don't bump into each other in the sky, or when they land. They also guide planes to their parking spaces.

Coming down
Pilots talk to air traffic control over the radio. They say they are on their way, and ask when and where to land.

Flight attendant

I am a flight attendant and one of the cabin crew on a passenger plane. My job is to care for passengers and to make them as comfortable as possible. I show them to their seats, tell them about safety, and where to find everything from film controls to magazines. I also serve them meals.

Before take-off
Before the flight starts, a flight attendant hands out newspapers or magazines, and checks that everyone has clicked their seat-belts shut.

Musician

guitar

metronome

I am a musician, a concert violinist, and I play my violin to audiences all over the world. I also record famous composers' music for CDs and television. Even when I'm not performing I have to practise every day, otherwise I don't play well.

Jazz instrument
Saxophones are used for jazz music. People go to clubs to hear them played by musicians.

conductor

Playing the violin
A violin makes music when a bow is moved over its four strings.

Orchestra at work
Up to 100 musicians sit on the stage when a symphony orchestra performs. Together they make a powerful sound that can fill the biggest concert halls. The musicians are guided through the music by a conductor. He makes sure they start playing at the right time.

trumpet

drums and cymbals

computerised keyboard

Making music last
When musicians want to record songs they go to a recording studio. They play or sing into a microphone. The songs are then recorded on tape, and copied on to CDs and cassettes.

Ballet dancer

At the barre
Dancers use a barre to balance as they exercise.

I am a ballet dancer and I belong to a ballet company in a big city. During the day I go to classes to rehearse new ballets, and in the evening I dance before a large audience. I wear beautiful costumes. I am very fit and supple, and I can dance for hours with hardly any rest at all.

In competition
Most ballroom dancers practise for months to perfect their moves.

principal dancers

ballet positions

tutu

Knowing where to stand
Each part of the stage has a name, and dancers follow stage directions. This is especially important when lots of dancers are on stage at once.

Traditional dance
Indian dancers dress in traditional costumes. When they dance, they move their heads, arms, hands, and bodies. These movements tell stories of great love or sudden and cruel death. Their dance is like the story-telling of ballets.

Ballet shoes
Pointe shoes have stiffened tips so that dancers can dance on their toes.

Accounting computers
Computers keep records of the money a firm spends. Records can be printed out as necessary.

Adding it up
Accountants use calculators to add up figures more quickly than they can in their heads.

Accountant

I am an accountant and I use numbers to make my living. My job is to keep track of all the money that comes in and goes out of my firm. I make sure that people who owe us money don't forget to pay. I also write cheques to pay the wages of the people who work with me, and keep petty cash for small office purchases.

petty cash

Lawyer

I am a criminal lawyer and I defend people who have been accused of a crime. I study the case and talk to any witnesses. Then I go to court with my clients. I try to prove my clients' innocence, and keep them out of jail.

Questioning a witness
Prosecution lawyers try to prove that a person is guilty. They need to show why, how, and when the accused committed the crime.

Stockbroker

I am a stockbroker and I buy and sell the shares of big companies. I try to buy shares when they are cheap. When the price goes up, I sell them and make a huge profit. I work hard, talking on the phone all day. I always try to avoid mistakes. Mistakes can cost lots of money.

international currency

Stock exchange
Hundreds of people meet to buy and sell shares at the stock exchange. Giant screens show how much the shares cost.

Trading shares
Most shares are traded by computer. Brokers work from screens that give them the latest prices. They type an order into their computer system when they want to buy or sell. It all happens very quickly.

pen

calculator

Full case
Stockbrokers must know what is happening in the world of business. They often carry newspapers and company reports in their briefcases.

Giving advice
Clients buy their shares with the help of an expert. But shares are risky – you can make money or lose it all.

Farmer

I am a farmer and I run a farm. I keep sheep for wool and cows for milk. I also grow wheat to make into flour. I get up early and start working as soon as it is light. I feed my animals and plough my fields. I work every day of the week.

Spring time
Farmers plough the fields ready for planting. Birds eat up any worms that are uncovered.

Cooped up
Chickens live in a coop and lay their eggs in straw. The eggs are collected and sold daily.

Cutting the wheat
Harvesters cut ripe wheat in the field. They separate the grain from the straw.

In the vineyards
Some farms grow grapes. The grapes are picked, then they are crushed and made into wine.

combine harvester

tractor and trailer

Sheep shearing
Sheep's wool is cut off to be made into clothes and blankets. Sheep look skinny afterwards.

Veterinary surgeon

I am a veterinary surgeon and I treat sick animals. I examine cats, dogs, and other small pets in my surgery. And if a cow or horse is unwell, I go by car to visit it on the farm. Then I give it medicine to make it well.

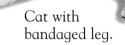
Cat with bandaged leg.

At the surgery
Pets wait in the waiting room for the vet to see them.

Vet visits
People carry their pets to the surgery in baskets so they don't run away.

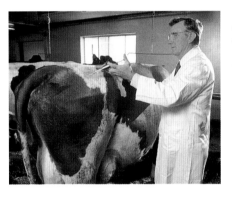

At the farm
Vets may treat whole herds of cows. To stop them catching and spreading an illness, they may all be injected on one day.

A sick cat
During a check-up, the vet asks how the animal is behaving. He then examines the animal to find out what is wrong.

Vets' instruments
Vets' instruments help them treat sick animals. Animals must keep still and not bite. To stop a dog biting, the vet may use a muzzle.

muzzle

ear torch

clippers

scissors

Difficult patients
Sometimes vets visit unusual patients in zoos. These animals may be too dangerous to treat when awake. Lions often have to be tranquillised first.

Postwoman

I am a postwoman and I deliver letters, parcels, and magazines. Well before dawn, while everyone is asleep, I'm up collecting mail from the post office. I fill my bag, then go out and deliver letters street by street.

Sorting mail
Post offices sort millions of letters a day by hand and by machine.

Letter boxes
People post their letters into post boxes. Each day the letters are collected and taken to the post office for sorting.

Stamps
Countries all over the world print their own stamps for people to buy.

letters

Post van
Letters and parcels are carried quickly across the country in vans. When parcels must be delivered the following day, they can be sent through private firms.

Rubbish collector

I am a rubbish collector and I drive a great big truck around the city streets. I go from house to house emptying dustbins into the back of my truck. I press a button and the rubbish is crushed so that it only takes up a small space. Then I take it to the dump and empty it out. I also collect newspapers and bottles that can be recycled.

At the dump
Bags of rubbish are pushed into holes. Later they will be covered with soil and plants.

Other clearing up
Oil has to be cleaned off beaches after an oil spill. This helps save wild birds and plants.

Collecting rubbish
Rubbish is collected weekly so it doesn't rot in the street.

Librarian

I am a librarian and I work in a library. I know a lot about books and sometimes I advise people on what is good to read. I stamp books when they are borrowed, and put them in the right place on the shelf when they are brought back. I also give people information about things that are happening in their neighbourhood.

book

Library computers
Information can be found on computers as well as in books.

On screen
Some people copy facts on to their own computers.

Shelves of books
Libraries hold thousands of books. Books on each subject are kept together to make it easy for customers to find what they want.

Editor

I am an editor and I make books, magazines, or newspapers. I check that the stories and pictures are right and that everything is printed on time.

In charge
Editors work with writers, photographers, designers, and illustrators. They all help to make a publication. Editors hold meetings and say who works on each story.

Designer

I am a designer and I try to set the fashion for the year ahead. I create clothes for men, women, and children. I choose the colours and material they are made from, and how they are put together. Sometimes I organise fashion shows where my designs are shown to buyers from all over the world.

drawing board

page layout

paint-brushes

paint

fabric samples

Designing packs

Designers also make up the way drink cans, boxes, and carrier bags look. They create lots of designs before the final version is chosen.

Designing homes

Interior designers plan what the inside of a shop or home will look like. They choose paint, curtains, and furniture.

Designing books

Graphic designers sit at drawing boards to work out how a page will look. They design on computers too.

Mechanic

I am a garage mechanic and I fix cars when they break down or have an accident. I give healthy cars their regular service too – I always check the lights and change worn tyres.

Metal repairs
Broken metal parts can be repaired by welding them together with a blow torch.

Other car workers
Car designers make a full-size clay model of a new car. This helps them see what their plans really look like, so they can smooth out any faults.

Engine work
Sometimes an engine needs lots of work. It can be lifted out of the car to make it easier to take apart.

Mechanics' tools
Mechanics have dozens of tools and spare car parts. They use them to make repairs, tighten bolts, and get cars going.

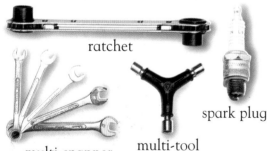

ratchet

multi-spanner

multi-tool

spark plug

screwdriver

Cover up
Cars are sprayed with paint for an even finish. The painters wear masks, gloves, and overalls so that they don't get soaked with paint.

Racing driver

At the start
Races begin with the cars lined up in rows, waiting for the green signal to go. The front drivers have the best chance to win.

I am a racing driver. I drive cars on racing tracks, and try to cross the finishing line before anyone else. I drive fast but with care – I don't want to have a crash. When I win, I am given a silver cup and plenty of applause. Sometimes I am interviewed for TV too.

Pit stop
When a driver pulls in and stops during a race, his mechanics set to work. They change all four tyres and refuel the car in a matter of seconds.

Racing trucks
When lorries race they move fast, but not nearly as fast as cars.

ear plugs

racing suit

gloves

boots

crash helmet

Formula one
These cars have upside-down wings that push them on to the road, and stop them taking off at high speeds.

Builder

I am a builder and I build the houses people live in. I dig the foundations and make the outside walls from bricks. Then I put in the windows and lay the floors. One of the last things I do is to plaster the inside walls.

drill

Building tall
Some builders put up big skyscrapers. They work high above the ground and build with steel and concrete.

hammer

screws

Plumber

I am a plumber and I work alongside builders. I fit water pipes, toilets, and baths, and connect them to the drains. I also clean out blocked pipes.

wrench

plunger

Painter

I am a painter. I decorate homes, shops, and offices. I have a van filled with pots of paints, ladders, and brushes. I always put down sheets when I work so carpets are not accidentally splashed.

roller

paintbrush

Painting a ship
When painters have to cover a large surface, such as the hull of a ship, they use spray guns.

Electrician

I am an electrician and I put in the wires that carry electricity around a building. I run wires beneath floors and behind walls so that all the lights work. Then I test the circuit to make sure it is safe.

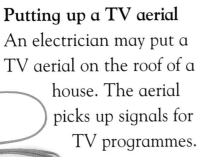

wire cutters

snips

Putting up a TV aerial
An electrician may put a TV aerial on the roof of a house. The aerial picks up signals for TV programmes.

Index

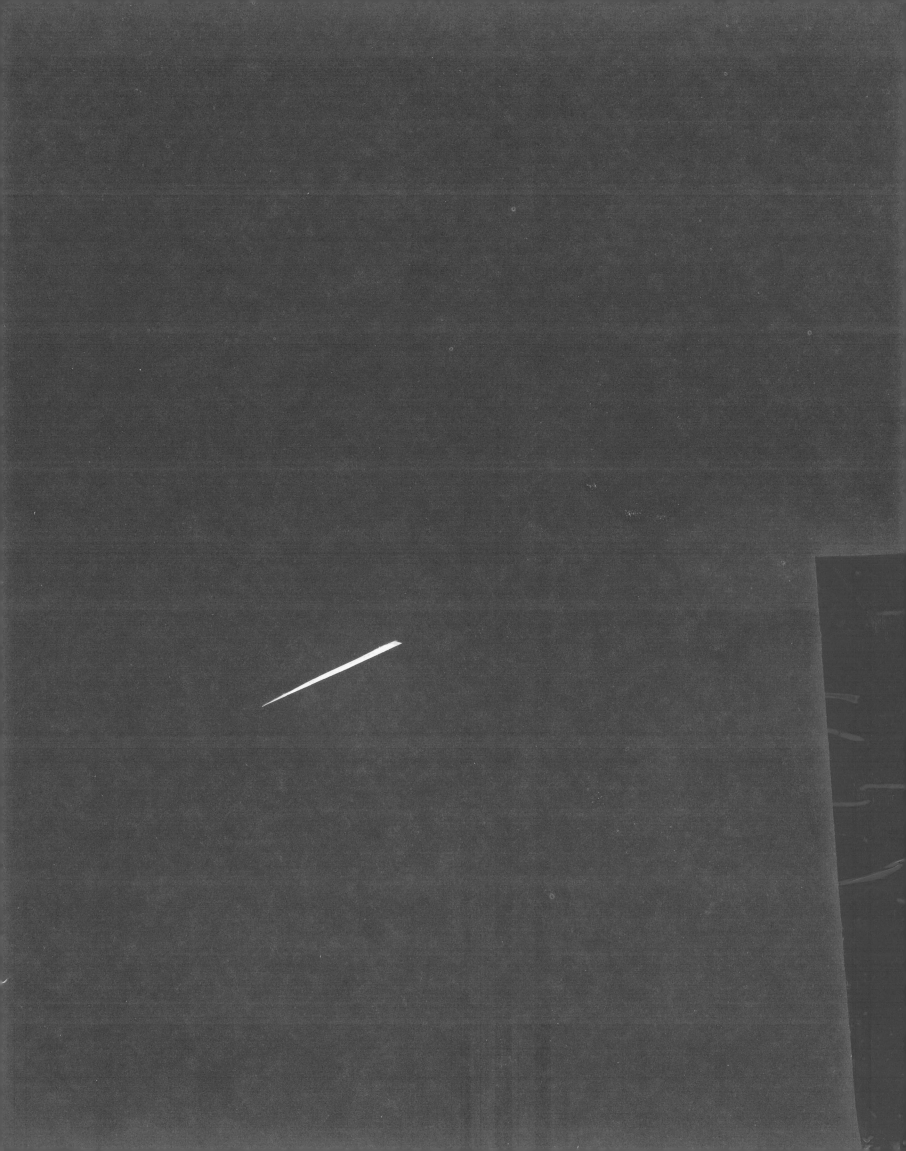